PORTRAIT

OF A

HOSPITAL

SURVIVOR

Gren

COLUMBUS BOOKS
LONDON

Other books in this series:
Portrait of a Golfaholic
(Mark Oman, illustrations by Gary Patterson)
Portrait of a Rugbyholic
(Gren)
Portrait of an American Footballer
(Gren)
Portrait of a TV Addict
(Gren)
Portrait of a Motorist
(Gren)

Copyright © 1989 Gren of the *South Wales Echo*

First published in Great Britain in 1989 by
Columbus Books Limited
19-23 Ludgate Hill, London EC4M 7PD

Designed by Rupert Kirby

Printed and bound by
The Bath Press, Avon

ISBN 0 86287 960 4

CONTENTS

Dedicated to the nursing staff at University
Hospital of Wales, Heath, Cardiff

1
WHAT IS A HOSPITAL SURVIVOR?

A hospital survivor is someone who refuses to be ground down by the hospital system, someone who has successfully side-stepped the boiled fish or mince in favour of a little delicacy prepared for him or her alone by a smitten doctor or nurse.

The hospital survivor does not wait outside the X-ray room, half-naked in the draughtiest corridor, while two young operators discuss the latest pop band.

Neither is he or she consigned to the boring corner-of-the-room bed from which he can't see that lovely nurse wobbling her way up the corridor; or she, the handsome doctor on his way to minister to her every need.

The hospital survivor has actually enjoyed his or her internment, and on the following pages we tell you how you too can turn the system to your advantage.

2
ON ARRIVAL AT HOSPITAL

As soon as you arrive at the hospital let the staff know that you are someone to be reckoned with. Whatever you do don't be prepared to sit around for hours in a plastic-coffee-cup-bedecked admittance room, clinging pathetically to a hospital form in one hand and a Tesco bag with your pyjamas etc. in the other.

Always try the positive approach: bang on the admittance counter with something heavy (a wallet always creates the greatest impression) as you await the attention of the down-market filing clerk masquerading as an admittance department senior executive. When she, with the air of her department's equivalent to Dr Christiaan Barnard, finally deigns to

acknowledge your existence, say something like
'Tell the ward I'm here and get someone to take
up my things. Ring my consultant. Tell him
where he can reach me and I want the *Telegraph*
and *Times* with my morning tea and bickies.'

The clerk, who by now thinks you're very
important, either on the hospital committee or
at the very least a born-again estate agent, will
soon have you up at your ward where the
hospital survival routine must now continue in
earnest.

This admission procedure applies to both
NHS and private hospitals. The only difference
is that in the latter the admittance clerk says
'please' now and again.

3
ENTERING YOUR WARD

———————

There's nothing patients like to see more than a new face on the ward. It gives them a chance to talk to someone else about their operations and yet another pair of eyes to flash their scars at. Their welcome to the ward is very genuine. Turn it, therefore, to your advantage, and as you breezily enter the ward introduce yourself to the patients, warmly shaking their hands (or, if you are in a ward of hand operations, their feet) while disguising the boredom you feel when they describe their individual ailments in tedious detail.

While doing all this, hint very vaguely from time to time that you are a great personal friend of the Minister of Health and the Chairman of the Hospital Board, or that you actually know Mr BUPA himself etc., etc. This sort of thing quickly percolates through to the nursing staff and puts you in a favoured position when it comes to important things – it could be that you are even asked which bed you would like to occupy.

4
WHICH BED SHOULD YOU OCCUPY?

You may think that the bed you occupy is of little importance. This is not so: it is second only in importance to you having the operation for which you went into the theatre.

Having the best bed in the ward is a great aid to a happy stay and therefore a speedy recovery, so have no qualms about turfing out some bed-bound patient who is linked up to complicated drips and electronic monitoring devices. Your bed position is important – go for it.

For the purposes of this illustration it must be assumed that you are in a largish ward of at least eight beds, not one of those boring little single-bed wards so beloved by private hospitals. (How can you possibly enjoy yourself in a small room with only enough room for you, your bed and a nubile nurse? Heigh-ho.)

After years of painstaking research we can confidently state that the only bed for the survivor is the one from which you can see down the corridor.

This position gives you the edge on all other patients, affording you those few extra seconds to hide from approaching unwanted visitors, enema-laden nurses and the odd person who thinks his presence will cheer you up.

5

CREATING THE RIGHT IMPRESSION

Once you have been offered a 'preferred' bed you must continue the illusion of being someone rather special by making an impression about your background. This you can do by the way you appear in your bed-wear.

For men: Monogrammed silk pyjamas should delicately complement your sleek regimental dressing gown whose breast badge hints at a rather superior Guards regiment (only on discharge do you admit to it being a Guinness bottle label). Your footwear should be either leather moccasins or silk-topped slip-ons.

Ladies too can create the right impression by being beautifully coiffured and skilfully made-up as they draw back the curtains and step into ward life with ostrich feathers ballooning from flowing silk Chinese robes.

Remember: the object is to impress. In so doing you will receive greater attention, and therefore your stay will be much more enjoyable.

6

BREAKING UP THE LONG, BORING DAYS

One of the most unacceptable parts of a hospital stay is the habit they have of waking you at six in the morning when you want to sleep, and telling you to settle down at nine p.m. when you're just about ready for a night on the town.

To counter this long, boring day you must organize day-time parties. For instance, halfway through the morning invite all members of your ward, patients, staff and anyone who may be passing for elevenses around your bed. Nothing complicated. A couple of bottles of sherry, a few gin-and-tonics and a bottle or two of medium white wine. Nuts and crisps are of course optional, and you and your guests (apart from one or two 'Nil by mouth' types) will find that the occasion soon becomes the main event of the ever more quickly passing day.

Often those with a competitive nature reciprocate by offering another little party around their beds at three and seven p.m. Always attend.

Never worry about having alcoholic drinks on your bedside locker: no one ever says you can't. You see notices about not spitting in the common room or not smoking unless in a designated area, but have you ever seen a notice saying 'no gin-and-tonics beyond this point'? No! Nor have we, therefore it must be allowed. And don't forget the old adage: someone who has a drink problem is someone who drinks almost as much as his doctor.

7

FLATTERY GETS YOU EVERYWHERE

Now that you've established yourself on the ward and the days are becoming enjoyable you should turn your attention to those wonderful nurses who are so helpful and ready to minister to your almost every need.

Now is the time to encourage them to be even more careful with you, especially in the department of injections. When one is due, compliment the nurse on the delicacy she displayed the last time she injected you. Explain that it must have taken great skill and practice to administer the needle in such a gentle and painless way as she succeeded in doing (even if you really thought she was like a demolition engineer in a hurry).

Soon, word will spread among those who may be giving you future injections that you are something of an authority on the subject and not wanting to appear any less able, other nurses will ensure the most loving treatment and will purr with delight as you compliment their efforts too.

This system does not only apply to injections. Try a similar thing with enemas, blood-pressure tests and blood sampling. Nurses love to feel that they are appreciated – let them know at every opportunity that they are.

8
CREEPING GENERALLY

Once you have perfected the 'flattery-improves-your-injections' technique you may soon realize that there is nowhere on earth where blatant creeping is better employed than within a hospital.

Anyone who is a serious hospital survivor will automatically creep round staff members from the humblest nurse to the top consultant. The system is always the same: up-rank those who can do you a favour, and talk to them as if they are much further up the favours ladder than they actually are.

A junior nurse, if referred to as 'sister', will accept your flattery with gratitude. So, too, with apprentice doctors. Call them 'Mister' and introduce them to your visitors as your consultant or specialist, and they too will respond in such a way as to ensure that they keep your high opinion.

Most people are unable to reject such flattering confidence in their assumed status. Soon you will find all sorts of unofficial favours coming your way. The odd trip for a drink in the staff bar and even a meal in the consultants' dining room could be the results of over-ranking.

Take advantage of such over-ranking. It works every time.

9
HOW TO COPE WITH HOSPITAL FOOD

Let's face it, although the kitchen staff try very hard, hospital food is always unappetizing. It's obviously impossible to prepare gastronomic delights for several hundred patients and a tea-bag will only go so far. You may as well face up to it: the highlight of your stay isn't going to be the food and drink.

The survivor has, of course, accepted this and within a day or two of admittance you should politely tell the big bosses in the kitchen department that, due to a rather embarrassing condition brought on by a rare tropical disease, you are forced to live on a special diet, of which they will be advised daily. This of course varies depending on your fancies and if properly managed you can easily find yourself nibbling lobster thermidor followed by a light tropical dessert and washed down with a bottle of vintage wine. (Here again use the aforementioned flattery technique. Ask the chap in the kitchen for his advice on which wine to serve with lobster.)

Serious survivors should however be advised to vary their diet. Lobster every day can lead to constipation and spots.

10
KEEPING THE MEDICAL STAFF AWARE OF YOUR PRESENCE

You must never be prepared to be just left to recuperate or for the experts to forget about you in the hope that your post-operation recovery will take its natural course. That's no way to enjoy your stay. Attention from the nursing staff is what you need for a proper recovery and this can be gained by periodically throwing them into panics.

One of the most effective ways to get love and attention from the nursing staff is to discover a rather nasty rash upon your person. Nurses hate rashes; they have a habit of spreading throughout the ward, then the whole hospital, and soon the staff have to be in work on their day off. Therefore they always react to a few spots.

The best way of getting a really panic-starting rash is to give yourself a long hot soak in the bath, ensuring that you are lying on the pimple side of the rubber bath mat. This, even after you've dried off, gives a most impressive rash, guaranteed to be the centre of attention for all on the ward. Even the most learned of consultants will be baffled, but by the time they've dealt with you your loving nurses will have gently powdered and massaged all the bits that aren't covered in spots. Also depending on how well you play things you could easily find yourself being plied with little goodies by one dolly nurse as another drops grapes into your mouth.

Your interesting condition will of course miraculously improve, much to everyone's amazement. This is of course the time for you to say loudly and often that you put it down to the skilful nursing and early diagnosis (not that, apart from the grapes, you've had any medication). This keeps everyone happy, the staff feel clever and you've had a wonderfully pampered afternoon.

It goes without saying that they will keep a special eye on you in case the condition returns. Don't use this ploy too often. Warm baths are weakening.

11
WHO'S WHO ON THE WARDS

To get the most out of your stay in hospital it's as well to be advised of who's who in the order of things. We know of some patients who have mistaken the person who comes to shave your interesting bits prior to an operation for the tea lady, resulting in very strange goings on when asked to 'leave one lump and stir it about a bit'. You see then why it's important that you know who's who, so that with the appropriate adjustment in your attitude you get the best out of them.

1. The tea lady.
You can hardly fail to recognize these ladies. They are the ones attached to huge food containers or large teapots. Always try to cultivate friendships with these ladies, as you never know when you'll need to swap what you ordered yesterday for something which looks a little more appetizing today.

2. The auxiliary nurse.

No ward could operate without the talents of the auxiliary. While staff nurses may be more qualified for the job, and student nurses younger and therefore quicker, the auxiliary nurse is the one who can actually *do* it.

3. The student nurse.
Always reading, studying or staggering back from some junior doctor's flat in the residential wing. They are very helpful and attentive but they always make you feel that you are a guinea pig.

43

4. The State Enrolled Nurse.

Let's not kid ourselves. The State Enrolled Nurses run the whole show. The sister and nursing officer may think they are in charge but it's the SENs who really put the show on the road.

Always look after this rank. They can influence your hospital life considerably.

5. The staff nurse.

This lady has a certain amount of authority, therefore she can help with ward favours i.e. she can be asked to smuggle in the odd bottle of gin and will often take you to secret 'smoking-is-allowed-here' areas of the hospital normally only frequented by doctors.

6. The sister.

Be careful here. Sisters can usually see through the barrage of 'flattery-will-get-you-anywhere' routines, so try a new approach. Lady patients may like to try the 'I think we are distantly related' routine while male members of the ward may like to try something like 'I find bloodshot eyes and the odd pimple sexually arousing.' If these fail try anything because a really great stay in hospital depends upon you making a friend of sister.

7. The nursing officer.

Don't worry too much about these: whether they are nursing officers, senior nursing officers or chief nursing officers, they won't have much effect on the quality of your ward life. If one should stray into your bed area smile sweetly and call her doctor, as that always seems to keep them happy.

8. The junior doctor.

Junior doctors or 'housemen' are recognizable because they keep dropping off to sleep at the bottom of your bed. This is due to them being terribly overworked. Most of them work 38 hours a day. Junior doctors also like walking about in ill-fitting, white buttonless coats, their pockets bulging with medical apparatus such as stethoscopes, little hammers, torch lights and X-ray machines.

9. The registrar.

These are doctors who can't decide if they're still one-of-the-boys doctors or aloof consultants. However, gain their friendship. They can often be relied upon to manufacture gin or vodka in the lab. if your supplies for the elevenses party run out.

10. The consultant.

You can easily spot this chap; he's the one in front when a group of medical people are walking around the wards. He is also the one who turns to his team of apprentice doctors with questions such as 'What would you say is wrong with this patient?', when he himself has been baffled by 'this patient' for weeks.

Some patients find they take an instant dislike to the manner of the consultant, but don't let such trivial matters influence you. Without the consultant on your side you stand no chance of a wonderful stay. Work on gaining his friendship. It's time well spent.

12

HOW TO GAIN SYMPATHY (AND BOXES OF CHOCOLATES)

Whatever you do never tell any fellow patients the full extent of the trouble for which you are hospitalized.

Don't forget, the whole object of this exercise is for you to get as much fun out of your stay as possible, and you will be much more popular in your ward if the others think you are laughing off a very serious, painful condition just to cheer them up.

Let slip now and again that you refuse to depress the whole ward by discussing your condition. Your attitude will be well received. Soon you (the martyr) will be admiringly offered bottles of nicely chilled wine (ten minutes in the liver transplantation chest unit does a medium white a treat) while others, as they are discharged, will leave their unopened boxes of chocolates, Lucozade and tins of biscuits to you. You, of course, generously pass on the Lucozade to the nurses.

In our continuing effort to help you really enjoy your stay, may we offer a few embellishments which will make the most insignificant complaint seem possibly terminal, in the hope of getting sympathetic reactions from all and sundry.

You say:	You mean:
It's a lump – they're deciding whether or not to operate.	I'm in for a boil on my bum.
There's something restricting my per-ambulatory system.	I've got an ingrowing toenail.
I get periodic amnesia which often leads to self-inflicted wounds.	I got thrown out of a strip club when I was drunk, so they tell me.
The consultant isn't even making a decision yet: he wants me to have time to think.	I'm constipated.

You say:	You mean:
They think I've been poisoned.	I've got a septic finger.
I may have to give up a very promising sporting career.	My dart rebounded and stabbed me in the foot.
Certain foreign bodies have been discovered in my respiratory system.	I've got a marble wedged up my nose.
The specialist has warned people that I should really be in an isolation ward.	I've got a wind problem.
I'm not allowed to talk about it, Official Secrets Act and all that. But it's something to do with germ warfare.	I've got a cold.
I'd really rather say no more than that I'm involved in pushing the boundaries of medical science to limits hitherto thought to be unreachable.	I'm having my piles done.

13
MEDIC-SPEAK

There is a language which is common to all hospitals. This is called Medic-speak. It is taught at all medical schools and it is intended to disguise what is really going on.

If you are going to enjoy your stay fully, it is essential that you should understand exactly what is meant by some standard medical phrases.

They say:	They mean:
How are we today?	How are you today?
It looks a little angry today.	God help you tomorrow.
You may feel slight discomfort.	It'll hurt like hell.
This may hurt a little.	This will hurt a lot.
All you'll feel is a slight prick on your thumb.	It will feel like I'm stabbing you with a javelin.

They say:	They mean:
Some patients dislike the flavour.	The vast majority find it totally unbearable.
We'll try to get you out of bed tomorrow.	If you don't get up we'll tip you out.
Nurse says you had a restful night.	You didn't keep her awake anyway.
You're looking better today.	Gee, you looked dead rough yesterday.
We'll be taking a decision on you today.	Heads it's mumps, tails it's shingles.
Have you opened your bowels recently?	Couldn't you be a bit more generous with the air freshener?

14
THE DAY OF YOUR OPERATION

It's only natural to contemplate your operation with a certain amount of anxiety. After all, there are more alcoholics within the medical profession than any other, so there's a fair chance that you'll be sliced open by some drink-sodden medic wearing a hat and singing 'I did it my way'. However, look on the bright side. A happy surgeon is a good surgeon, eh?

There really is no need for you to fear the operation. What you must do is make the occasion the high point of your stay. To do this is very easy. Just open a book on your operation: offer evens on the exact time you leave the ward and the exact time you return, how long you are actually in the theatre and the number of stitches you have. Sometimes on really large wards the money is considerable and reports of Ladbroke's and Coral trying to muscle in on such business are not without a basis of truth.

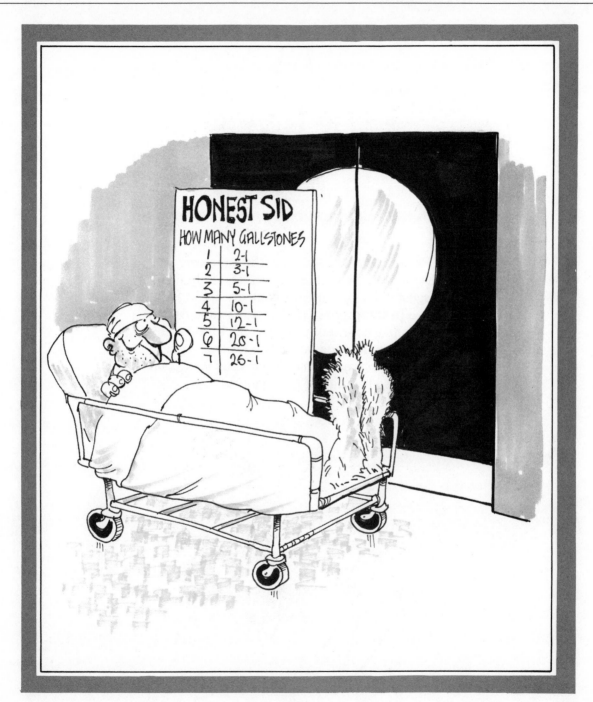

Properly organized, you, the survivor, can always win. This is done with the help of your surgeon who can always control things for a share in the profits. However, beware BUPA surgeons who often enter the book under an assumed name and scoop the lot.

Ah yes, correctly organized your operation can be the fun day of the year.

15

ALWAYS MAKE A PROFIT

This applies more to the ladies' wards than it does to the men's. First of all you must be aware of the possibilities of there being money to be made out of your fellow patients, and it's a well known fact that if ladies are hospitalized for more than two days they develop shopping withdrawal syndrome. This must of course be pandered to.

Have you ever met a woman in hospital who was satisfied with her slippers, nightdress, negligee or dressing gown? Of course not, so what better time to let it be known that you have access to large chain store seconds of such apparel. You take their orders and get someone (probably sister, whom you have corrupted earlier) to buy whatever is required from a back-street market. Add 100 per cent for profit and they think you're doing them a great favour.

Cosmetics, too, can be a nice little earner while you are on the ward. Just kit yourself out with the latest from the Avon people and you're straight in with a profit.

Don't forget, either, that Tupperware parties on the ward are profitable and fun, but don't get too greedy. Hospital authorities hate having to organize two ambulances just to take one gift-laden lady patient home.

There are of course many profit-making schemes you may like to try. Some that our research has shown to be highly profitable are as follows:

1. Photograph your friends in their very own hospital beds, with or without nurses or doctors; £3 per print.

2. Supply soft and alcoholic drinks, sandwiches, pork pies, crisps etc. 24-hour service for large profits.

3. Read people to sleep, or through-the-night service. Charge per quarter-hour – read anything except hospital romances.

4. Push patients' wheelchairs around the ward, corridors or grounds. Prices on application.

5. Talk to your friends' unwanted and boring visitors. £5 per hour.

16
A LAST-NIGHT PARTY

When you have decided that you are well enough to leave the hospital (see next chapter), always arrange a bring-a-bottle party. You will of course arrange to supply your guests' bottle needs, at a price.

Send out invitations to everyone who has in any way helped to make your stay enjoyable.

When the guests start to congregate around your bed, play host or hostess with great appreciation of their presence, offering around the odd bedpan full of salted nuts and a dentures dish of crisps as you encourage them to drink lots of the stuff they have brought (via yourself) with them.

The reason for this show of affection from you is of course to give your hospital friends the opportunity to deluge you with little prezzies, which you gratefully accept with all the sincerity you can muster. A really good last-night party can produce a very healthy profit.

17
DECIDING WHEN TO LEAVE HOSPITAL

You may be under the impression that you are told by someone in authority when it is time for you to leave hospital. This is of course completely untrue. You are the best judge of your condition, so it's quite sensible that you should be the only judge as to the day of your departure.

Why leave when you are enjoying yourself so much? Why leave when there may be several fiddles that you haven't even tried out yet? The practised hospital survivor will always time his or her departure perfectly. You should aim to

strike a perfect balance between recovery and being rumbled by your colleagues.

You may like to try some or all of the following ruses which may help to give you an extended stay.

1. Put shaving cream around your mouth and roll on the floor screaming for sister. (Worth an extra week.)

2. Stage a fall and crash into the tea trolley. Feign broken ankle. (Extra five days.)

3. Try the bath-mat ploy again. (Two days.)

4. Propose marriage (or something similar) to sister. (The number of days you gain by this depends on sister.)

5. Hide in laundry room. (One day.)

6. Hide in laundry room with staff nurse. (One week.)

7. Have a mouthful of hot coffee when they take your temperature prior to you leaving. (Three days extra.)

8. Feign loss of memory, i.e. you can't remember where you live. (This can last indefinitely.)

18
FOND
FAREWELLS

When you decide it's time for you to leave, do it with style. Arrange for someone to pack all your presents, various ill-gotten gains and personal belongings into a waiting taxi while you make a farewell tour of those who have made your stay such a pleasant one. Depending upon your nature shake hands with, hug or kiss those you are leaving behind, not forgetting doctors, nurses and administration staff.

Perhaps at a time like this you are lost for words. If this is the case you may like to try some of the following friendly and comforting remarks.

'Goodbye, Herbert. I'll never tell anyone what you're being treated for, honest.'

'Thanks for everything, nurse; I'm sure sister won't report you for it, but if she does I'll tell her I talked you into it.'

'Don't worry, Doris, no one takes any notice of such innocent perversions these days.'

'Thanks for your company, Ronald. I really hope they find a cure for it soon.'

'All the best. I'll be back in to see you in a week if it's not too late.'

'Goodbye, sister. Don't worry, your drink problem secret is safe with me.'

'Thanks, staff nurse. In case you were worried, I didn't see anything going on in the laundry room that night between you and that young doctor.'

Then you're gone, off into the sunset after enjoying your stay, wondering when you'll be lucky enough to have the company of such lovely people again.

As they say in medical jargon, 'Get Well Soon.'

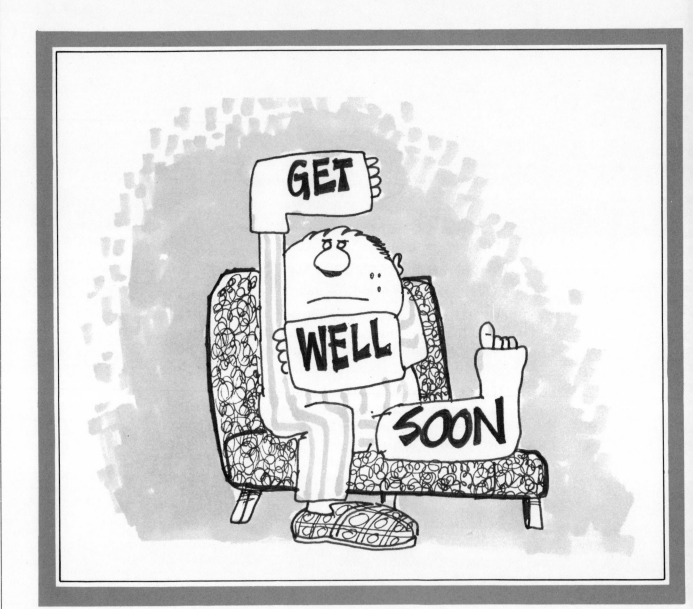